William Henry Furness

**Folk-lore in Borneo**

A Sketch

William Henry Furness

**Folk-lore in Borneo**
*A Sketch*

ISBN/EAN: 9783744768894

Printed in Europe, USA, Canada, Australia, Japan

Cover: Foto ©Andreas Hilbeck / pixelio.de

More available books at **www.hansebooks.com**

A Kayan Chief.

# FOLK-LORE IN BORNEO

## A SKETCH

BY

WILLIAM HENRY FURNESS 3D, M.D., F.R.G.S.

MEMBRE DE LA SOCIÉTÉ DE GÉOGRAPHIE À PARIS
MEMBER OF THE AMERICAN PHILOSOPHICAL SOCIETY
MEMBER OF THE AMERICAN ORIENTAL SOCIETY

[*PRIVATELY PRINTED*]

WALLINGFORD
DELAWARE COUNTY, PENNSYLVANIA
1899

# A SKETCH

# FOLK-LORE OF BORNEO.

In this short monograph I do not pretend to give anything
more than a Sketch of the Folk-lore to be found among the
Borneans. The island is large, and the people, scattered and
isolated by constant inter-tribal warfare, differ one tribe from
another, in language, customs and appearance almost more than
do Germans, French, or English ; to say that any tradition or
custom is common to all the tribes, or even to all of one tribe, of
Borneans, would be far too sweeping. A still greater drawback
to any universality, in legend or custom, is that there is no writ-
ten language, not even so much as picture-drawings on rocks
to give us a clue to ancient myths or traditions. The natives   •
of Borneo are in a certain sense savages, but yet they are savages of a high order, possessed of a civilization far above what
is usually implied by the term ; they live together in what almost
might be called coöperative communities, they practise the art of
weaving, they forge rough implements of iron, they cultivate rice
and esculent plants, and in all their work, such as house-build-
ing, boat-building, manufacture of cloth and weapons of warfare,
they show an ambitious desire, and a skilful ability, to ornament

their work and add, to its usefulness, pleasure to the eye.  One of -their gravest faults, however, is their embarrassing tenacity to the *fad* of head-hunting, and a strict adherence to the principle of an eye for an eye and a tooth for a tooth.  This keeps the different households, even of the same tribe, at constant war and makes inevitable an uncomfortable yet pleasing interchange of heads during the tedious months of the rainy season, when time hangs heavy on the warriors' hands, and disused swords might get rusty.

So little is known of the social and anthropological position of these people, to others than those who make Malaysia and the South Sea islands their study, that it may not be out of place to give a short description of the people themselves before entering on the subject of their Folk-lore.

The remote origin of the Borneans, as well as of the greater part of all of the inhabitants of the Polynesian islands, is an ethnological problem; they are not Malay, neither are they Mongolian nor Negrito; they bear resemblances here and there to all of these races, but not marked enough to claim any one as the parent stock.  Furthermore, there is some evidence in favor of the theory that they are the result of successive migrations of tribes from northern India and from Anam.

The inland tribes of Borneo, by which I include all the natives except the Malays settled along the coast, are without any definite forms of religious worship; they make idols of wood, but I have never seen any offering made to them, nor do they regard them apparently as anything more than as scarecrows to frighten off evil spirits.  They are the children of Dame Nature and as such have inherited their mother's disregard for life, and this feature of their temperament has kept them in a constant

A Kayan Long-House.

turmoil of warfare, which in turn compels them for mutual protection to band together in communities of several families and build for themselves a common house wherein to live, ever ready to turn out in force and resist the attacks of hostile tribes. In not a few instances these houses are as much as a quarter of a mile in length and shelter as many as four hundred people. Every household is presided over by a head-man known as the elder, or *Orang Tuah*, and he in turn is governed in a measure by the chief of the tribe, known as the *Penghulu*. The government of the household seems to be conducted in the quietest manner; I have lived on several occasions in these houses for three or four weeks at a time, and have never seen anything that could be called a violent quarrel between two members of the household, nor have I seen the Orang Tuah or the Penghulu submit any of the members to what might be considered harsh treatment. I have also been with them when they were out on the warpath, to use a North-American Indian term, when every nerve was at high tension on the look-out for enemies and every thought was turned to slaughter, but I have never seen the counsel of the Chief disregarded. Of course, some Chiefs are weak and fail to give commands because they are afraid to act, but a command once given is carried out, or at least not disregarded, and I could never detect any means which were taken to enforce an authority thus implicitly obeyed.

As a people, they are not active-minded nor industrious, but yield to the influence of climate, and, following the example offered to them by the vast, dense jungle on every side, accept life as easily as it comes. They are no exception to the rule that all untutored minds, living in constant communion with any awful aspect of Nature, be it gigantic mountains, a waste of waters, or an illimitable jungle, are saturated with superstitions; every pool, every tree, every rock is the home of an evil spirit, and all mysterious noises in the forest are ghostly whisperings. Everywhere are signs and omens to warn man of danger or direct his course; theirs is a life where no schooling is so vital as the ability to read aright the "sermons in stones, books in the running brooks." For them the world is the patch of jungle covering the few square miles that they know, and bounded by the hills in the distance; seldom do they get an extended view of the surrounding country; trees hem them in on all sides and the mountains are so difficult of ascent, and furthermore so infested with demons or "antu," that the summits can be gained only at the risk of body, and, still worse, of soul.

Many natives of the interior live and die with never a glimpse of the sea, and the tales which the Malay and Chinese traders tell of lands beyond the horizon where white men live, are as incomprehensible to them as are to us the conjectural accounts which astronomers give of the canals on the planet Mars.

Naturally enough, of course, creation began on the island of Borneo, or Kalamantan, as they call it, and the first people were Borneans and spoke the language of the tribe that tells the story. Every tribe has a different account of creation, and claims that its people sprang from the first created mortals. The following account is the story of Genesis according to the Kayans of Northwestern Borneo:—

In the old, old days, when there was nothing but water and sky, there fell from the heavens an enormous rock; that part of it which protruded from the water was hard, slippery, and quite bare, with no soil nor plants upon it of any kind. After a long time, however, the rains produced slime upon the rock, and little worms, called *halang*, were bred in this slime, and they bored into the rock and left fine sand outside of their burrows; this sand eventually became soil and covered the rock. Again years passed and the rock remained barren of all other life until suddenly there dropped from the Sun a huge wooden handle of a *Parang* (or sword) known as *Haup Malat*. This parang-handle sank deep into the rock and taking root in the soil it sprouted and grew into a great tree, named *Batang Utar Tatei*, whose branches stretched out over the new land in every direction. When this tree was fully grown, there dropped from the Moon a long rope-like vine known as the *Jikwan Tali*. This vine quickly clung to the tree and took root in the rock. Now the vine, Jikwan Tali, from the Moon became the husband of the tree, Batang Utar Tatei, from the Sun, and Batang Utar Tatei gave birth to twins, a male and a female, not of the nature of a tree, but more or less like human beings. The male child was called *Klobeh Angei*, and the female was called *Klubangei*. These two children married and then gave birth to two more children, who were named *Pengok N'gai*, and *Katirah Murai*. Katirah Murai was married to old man *Ajai Avai*, who comes without pedigree into the narration. From Katirah Murai and Ajai Avai are descended many of the chiefs who were founders of the various tribes inhabiting the land of Kalamantan; their names are Sejau Laho, Oding Lahang, from whom the Kayans spring, Tabalan, Pliban, and, finally, Tokong, the father of head-hunting.

As time went on, that which formerly had been merely slime on the rock, became moss, and little by little small plants were produced. The twigs and leaf-like appendages of the tree, evidently the female principle in nature, as they fell to the ground, became birds, beasts, and fishes. (Let me mention here that the endowment of leaves with life and locomotion is no more than natural; while in the jungle I have repeatedly seen what, in every respect, appeared to be a leaf fall to the ground and then miraculously put out legs and walk away; it was one of those remarkable insects of the *Mantis* family, or "walking leaves.") The inhabitants of the rock had no need of fire in those days, for the sun beat down on them strongly, and there was no night; it was not until many, many years had elapsed that an old man named *Laki Oi* invented a method of obtaining fire by means of friction produced by pulling a strip of rattan rapidly back and forth beneath a piece of dry wood. This process of making fire he called *Musa*, and it is still the only method used in obtaining fire for ceremonials, such as the naming of a child, or when communicating with the omen-birds. Laki Oi also taught them the use of the fire-drill, which he called the *Nalika*.

On the main trunk of Batang Utar Tatei was a large excrescence, from which exuded a resinous gum called *Lutong*, which, as it dropped to the ground beneath, was immediately transformed into chickens and swine; and it is because they were thus formed out of the very heart and substance of the tree that they are always used in the reading of auguries. From this same cause, there was innate in them an insight into the innermost workings of Nature and a knowledge of the future.

The first beings with any resemblance to man had neither legs, nor breasts, and consisted merely of a head, chest, arms, and a fragment of a body which hung down in shreds and rags, having the appearance of twisted snakes. When they moved they dragged themselves along the ground by their arms. (From this description and from native carvings, I am inclined to believe that a large cuttle-fish or octopus must have suggested this idea to the original narrator of this tradition.) Little by little, the body was brought into more compact form, and, in a later generation, legs appeared, but it was a long time before they became accustomed to legs and able to use them in moving about. A survival of this awkwardness, so say the Kayans, is still noticeable in the way in which children crawl about the floor, and in their clumsy walk when first they learn to stand upright. The heads of these first people were, furthermore, much larger than the heads of the present generation, and, since it was the first part formed, it is the oldest part of the body, and on this account the most important member, and valued accordingly whether dead or alive.

This account is, as far as I know, purely Bornean, inasmuch as had there been any admixture from a foreign source (as we shall see further on was probably the case with the Dyaks) there would have been possibly some reference to a Supreme Creator rather than to this union of a vine and a tree as the original source of life. The Kayans from whom I obtained this account have had exceedingly little communication with the outside world, except through occasional Malay or Chinese traders. There is just a possibility that the idea of the wooden sword-handle being the ultimate *fons et origo* of all life comes from the fact that the word for chief—" penghulu "—is derived from "hulu," meaning a sword-handle, and the prefix "peng" denoting agency, so that the whole word means literally "the master of the sword," and thus the ruler or chief. From association of ideas, the sword-handle, without which the blade is ineffective and useless, may have been suggested to them as the chief of all beings. The sudden appearance of Ajai Avai on the scene as the husband of Katirah Murai, is not at all at variance with the accounts from many other sources of the populating of the world. In Laki Oi, we recognize the Kayan "Prometheus," whose memory is revered by sanctifying the fire procured after his manner of teaching, and from this tradition it is probable that the procuring of fire by means of the "fire-saw" is the aboriginal method. Should all of the fires in a Kayan house become extinguished and no spark be left, new fires may be started by this method, and by this method alone; even the fire-drill, and flint and steel, which are not unknown to them, are tabooed.

The Dayaks, who are closely akin in every respect to the Malays, and no doubt adopted the traditions which were rife among the Malays both before and after the latter became converted to Mohammedanism, give an account of the creation of the world differing in every particular from the foregoing Kayan story.

One of the Dayak versions of the creation which I heard from the people of that tribe, living in the Baram district of Sarawak, is that in the beginning there were two large birds,—the *Burong Iri* and the *Burong Ringgong* (Burong meaning *bird*), who made all the rivers, the great sea, the earth, and the sky. The first things to have life were plants and trees. When trees were first made, the winds blew them down, and again and again the Iri and the Ringgong had to set them up, until in their great wisdom they realized the necessity of props and stays, so they fashioned the strong vines and creepers. Then these two creators saw what pleasant places the boughs and branches of these trees would make for other beings; whereupon they created birds and all flying animals, like bats and flying squirrels. Then for a long while they consulted together, and, finally, decided that they would make a man who should walk about on the earth ; at first, they made him of clay, but when he was dried he could neither speak nor move, which provoked them, and they ran at him angrily; so frightened was he that he fell backward and broke all to pieces. The next man that they made was of hard wood, but he, also, was utterly stupid, and absolutely good for nothing. Then the two birds searched carefully for a good material, and eventually selected the wood of a tree known as the *Kumpong*, which has a strong fibre and exudes a quantity of deep red sap, whenever it is cut. Out of this tree they fashioned a man and a woman, and were so well pleased with this achievement that they rested for a long while and admired their handiwork. Then they decided to continue creating more men ; they returned to the Kumpong tree, but they had entirely forgotten their original pattern, and how they had executed it, and they were therefore able to make only very inferior creatures, which became the ancestors of the *Maias* (the Orang Utan) and monkeys.

The man and the woman were very helpless and hardly knew how to obtain the simplest necessities of life, so the Iri and the Ringgong devised the *Ubi*—a wild sweetpotato—the wild Tapioca, the Kaladi, or, as we know it, the Kaladium, and other edible roots, whereof the man and woman soon learned to eat ; fire, however, was unknown to these first people and they had to eat all of their food raw.

Contemporaneously with the Maias and the monkeys many other animals came into being, among them the dog. For a long time all living things were friendly to one another and lived in the land of Kaburau, which lies near a branch of the great Kapuas river, and is, even to this day, considered by the Dayaks as the garden-spot of the world. The dog, however, because he cleaned himself with his tongue, soon came to be despised by all other animals, and although a bully he was yet subservient to man. Then the deer and many of the other animals taunted the dog, saying that he was so mean-spirited and servile that although man thrashed him, nevertheless he fawned upon him and followed after him; which they would never do, so they went off to the jungle to live. But the dog comforted himself by saying that "When the man is about to strike me I crouch down and sometimes this keeps his hand off; furthermore, I cannot live on the poor food that these others must eat." Hence, the dog follows and obeys man.

One day when the man and the dog were in the jungle together, and got drenched by rain, the man noticed that the dog warmed himself by rubbing against a huge creeper, called the *Aka Rarah*, whereupon the man took a stick and rubbed it rapidly against the Aka Rarah, and to his surprise obtained fire. This was the origin of the *Sukan*, or fire drill, and ever after the man had fire in his house. Not long after, in accidentally dropping an Ubi near the fire, he found that it became much more pleasant to the taste; by this accident cooking was discovered.

In the course of time, the dog and other animals began to multiply, and man imitated their example; the woman brought forth a male child, whose name was *Machan Buntu*. After many years, the woman gave birth to a female child who, when she was well grown, married her brother Machan Buntu and gave birth to seventy children at one time. These children left

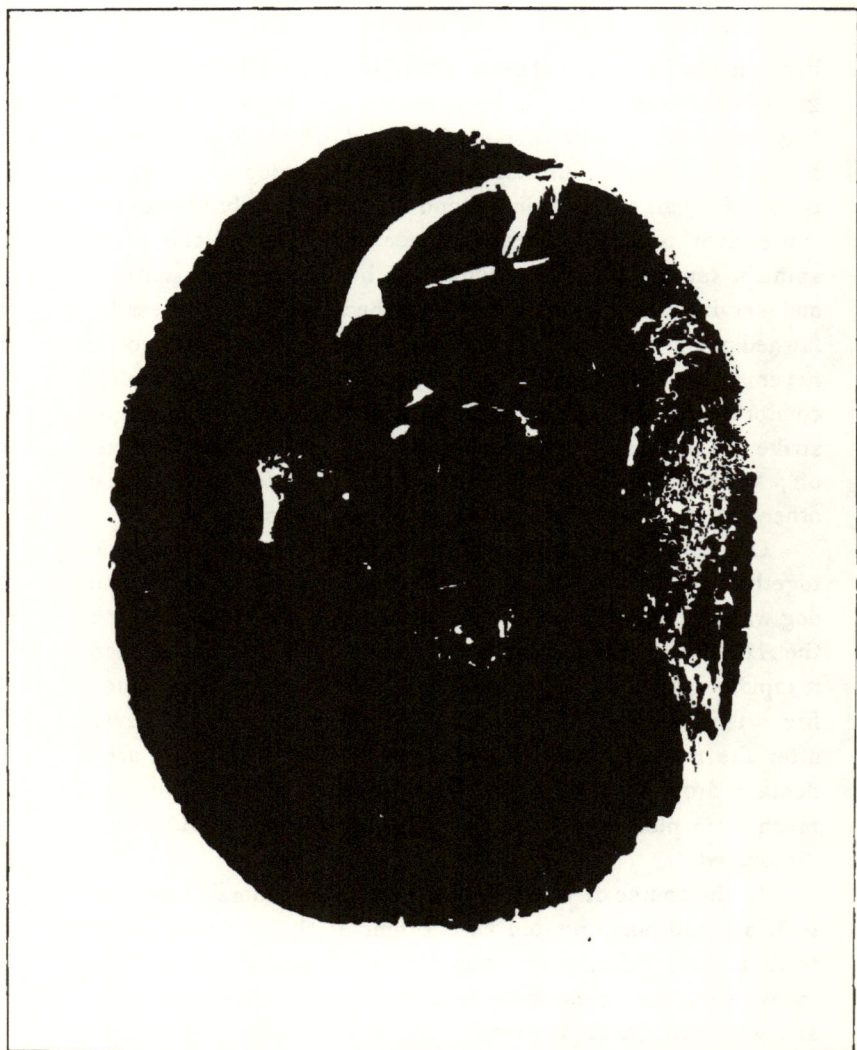

their home and scattered all over the world. Some became wood sprites and mountain gnomes, living in the trees, in the rivers, and under ground.

The tradition of the manufacture of man out of wood instead of clay is thoroughly in keeping with an origin purely Dayak. The Dayaks never have been proficient in pottery, and to this day they carve their bowls and dishes out of hard wood, otherwise it seems to me that clay would have suggested itself to them as the most suitable substance whereof to have made man. Another item looks as if part of the story were an interpolation, namely, where it is related that the two birds were so pleased with their work after making man, that they rested; this looks like a suggestion due to the first chapter of Genesis. Again, in that land of Kaburau, where all animals lived in perfect harmony, and which was the garden of the world, we may recognize the garden of Eden. Owing to the lack of writing, as I said before, it is impossible to say how old this tradition is, or to what extent it is known to Dayaks in other parts of the country; I have heard that very much the same story is told by the natives in the Rejang district several hundred miles south of the Baram; where the chiefest difference in the accounts is that earlier and higher than the birds there was a Supreme Being called *Rajah Gantalla*, who after creating the two birds, committed the rest of the work to them. I think in the -*allah* of this name (I speak under correction) we may discern a strong indication of Mohammedan influence. The first man, instead of being carved entirely of Kumpong wood, was made, in this latter account, of clay and then filled with the sap of the Kumpong tree.

A tradition (I do not say "legend," for this implies writing) which all the Kayans seem to know and to take pleasure in relating, is connected with the origin of their rite of head-hunting, for, although every possible means is employed by the European rulers of the island to stop this custom, it is still, nevertheless the one ruling passion of the people. Nay, it is part of their Religion; no house is blest which is not sanctified by a row of human skulls, and no man can hope to attain to the happy region of Apo Leggan unless he, or some near relative of his, has added a head to the household collection. Let me correct, however, with regard to head-hunting, what is probably the prevalent idea that the heads are hung up in the houses bleeding and raw, just as they are severed from the body. This is quite wrong; whether or not they would tolerate in their homes such horrid objects I cannot say, but certain it is that the heads are first subjected to fire and smoke until the flesh has dropped away, and what is then hung up is merely a skull; unpleasant enough, but not so bad as is generally supposed.

The tradition is that the great chief Tokong, when out on a war expedition, was told by Kop, the frog, that he should always take, instead of only the hair, the whole head of his enemies; Tokong was angry, at first, at the frog, but his followers at length persuaded him to let them try the experiment on their next attack. After taking the whole heads, the war party retreated quickly to the river down which they had come, and came to the spot where they had left their boats and were surprised to find that everything was exactly as they had left it. When they embarked, lo, and behold! the current of the stream was, for their sakes, reversed and like a flash they were carried up-stream and reached their home in a miraculously short time. During the fifteen days that they had been absent the crop of rice

A KAYAN YOUTH.

had not only sprouted, but had grown, had ripened, and was almost ready to be harvested; the members of their family who had been sick when they left, were now all well, the lame could walk and the blind see. The wise men waggled their heads, and one and all declared (and who can blame them?) that ever after they would stick to the custom that Kop had taught them.

It is not unfair to infer from this tradition that they have a crude, germinal sense of the barbarity of their actions, in so far as they think it necessary to invent an excuse to palliate that savage love of trophy-hunting which seems inborn in mankind. The rite of head-hunting is by no means confined to Borneo; the Formosans, and also many of our new fellow-citizens, among the tribes of the Philippines, are enthusiastic head-hunters, and our own cherished Indians within our own borders have not yet given up their love for a scalp; it would be perilous to assert that it is not a United States custom.

The idea that the taking of a head is necessary in order to obtain entrance to the pleasant regions of the land of departed spirits, is a doctrine taught by the chiefs in order to make men brave in battle, and do all in their power to avoid the punishment which awaits the coward. The Kayan Hades is believed to be under ground, and like the Hades of the ancient Greeks there is a guide to the entrance who corresponds to a certain extent to Charon. But their river Styx is not a stream, but a deep and wide ditch, through which flow ooze and slime swarming with worms and maggots; the souls of the departed must cross over this ditch not by a ferry, but by means of a fallen tree-trunk, guarded by the great demon *Maligang*, who challenges all comers, and if they have no record of bravery, he shakes the tree-trunk until they fall into the ditch below and are eternally tortured by the devouring worm that dieth not. Over the land of spirits presides the great demon *Laki Tenangan,* who assigns the souls to their proper place, and sees that they get their deserts, whether good or bad.

In this shadowy world, APO LEGGAN is one of the principal regions, and is the abode of the spirits of those who die from sickness or from old age. The souls in *Apo Leggan* have much the same lot as they had in this world; the poor remain poor, and the rich maintain their rich estate, and even the soul that has been harassed in life in the upper air must none the less expect to find misfortune and perplexity in the world to come. In the absence of any definite code of morals, this is, perhaps, the most suitable belief that a savage tribe could have ; it stimulates them to a constant endeavor to better their condition in this life and make their mark in some way, so that the life to come, in which they have a firm belief, may not be a continuation of the hardships they have endured here. Their methods of gaining wealth may not conform to our ideas of propriety, but then all is fair in love and war, and as they have very little idea of love, their motto has to be "all is fair in war;" life in the jungle is little else than a ceaseless struggle for the survival of the fittest.

LONG JULAN, a second division, is where live the souls of those who have died a violent or sudden death, either on the battlefield, or in their own clearings by the accidental fall of a tree ; and there also dwell the young mothers who have died in childbirth ; they become the wives of young warriors who likewise have been cut off in the bloom of youth and are therefore proper mates for unfortunate little mothers. Such beliefs naturally tend to the taking of life ; a young man, for instance, who loses his wife in childbirth wishes to meet her again in the next world, and his ambition to go on the warpath is doubly strong. Is he fortunate enough to take a head, he gains high rank among warriors ; should he be killed, he has the comfortable assurance that he will again meet his wife in *Long Julan*. The souls in *Long Julan* have an easy time and are always fairly well off, whatever their circumstances were in this life.

TAN TEKKAN, a third division, is the place to which Laki Tenangan consigns suicides; wretched and woe-begone in appearance, their souls wander about in the jungle and in the clearings trying to pick up a living by eating what roots and fruits they can find. This joyless Hereafter is calculated to make those who contemplate suicide, rather perform some self-sacrificing act of bravery whereby they will not only benefit those whom they leave behind, but also gain for themselves a more pleasant position in the world to come; therefore suicide is not at all common.

TENYU LALU, a fourth region, is assigned to the spirits of still-born children. These little souls are said to be exceedingly brave and need no other weapon wherewith to defend themselves than a stick of wood ; they have never felt pain nor experienced danger in this world, and are therefore totally ignorant of such emotions. Whether or not they increase in size in *Tenyu Lalu* is not known, but it is generally supposed that they live together in a little world of their own.

Finally, LING YANG is the abode of those who have died by drowning; it lies below the beds of rivers, and here the spirits soon become exceedingly rich. All the goods lost in rivers by the capsizing of boats in the rapids, or when they run foul of a snag in deep water, go into the coffers of the dwellers in *Ling Yang*.

Such are the main divisions of the *Dali Matei,* or country
of the dead; there are, however, many sacred hills, rivers,
and lakes wherein dwell certain powerful demons who govern
the spirits. In this nether world, some say that there are
trees and plants and animals much the same as in this; this
point, however, seemed open to considerable doubt in the minds
of some whom I questioned, while others had so definite an
idea of it that they drew maps to show the positions of the
different regions. They seemed to regard it as a large river,
along whose tributaries dwelt the various classes of departed
spirits. The Dayongs, or medicine men, are the only ones who
are supposed really to know; these all maintain that, while
acquiring their power over sickness, they had visited the land
of spirits. In the mythology of all countries there is sure to be
a hero who has made the descent to Hades and returned to tell
the tale, and the Kayans are no exceptions; they have their
Orpheus, only his name is Gamong.

Gamong, during an attack of fever, realized that he was at
the point of death, but was loath to resign his spirit, so he called
his friends around him and begged them to dress him up, after
death, in all his war-clothes, and not to bury him for three days,
but to place him in a sitting posture with his sword and spear in
his hands. He comforted them by saying that he had an inner
assurance that he had a terrible encounter before him, but that
he would actually return to this world in about three days.
Shortly after this, his breath ceased and his friends performed
all the rites of burial, just as he had requested. For three days
his body remained rigid; at the end of that time, he came back
to life and told his open-eyed friends his adventures as follows:
" When my spirit left you, I went directly down the path which

leads to the great tree-trunk, *Bintang Sikopa*, where Maligang
stands; according to his wont, he hailed me and told me to halt,
which I would not do.   Then Maligang, whose arm is enormous,
many times bigger than his body, began to shake the tree, call-
ing out 'who are you?' I replied 'I am Gamong, a brave
warrior, and you must not shake the tree while I cross.'   Maligang then said, consulting the pegs with which he records the
deeds of men, 'What proof have I that you have been brave?'
At this I was furious, I drew my parang, uplifted my spear and
ran amok, rushing into Maligang's house, smashing everything
and overturning the great jars of rice-toddy, of which there is an
abundance, but whereof no one ever drinks.   Maligang was
frightened and bolted from the house, shouting as he fled, 'I
have not got you now, but in seven years' time you must return.'   Finding that Maligang had fled, and that there were
other obstacles to prevent me from going on, I returned to this
world and its trials."   The story goes that Gamong lived seven
years after this, and then succumbed body and soul to the great
Maligang; and as there is no record of his bravery, he was probably shaken off of the tree-trunk and disappeared in the deep
pit seething with maggots.

All this veracious history I got by word of mouth from a
Kayan of the Tinjar valley.

Almost every medicine man has been down among the
spirits of the dead, and in proof of his assertions, a curiously
shaped stone, or a knot of wood, is displayed, which has been
given by the spirits and is endowed with all sorts of mar-
vellous properties.   I have in my possession a Dayong's whole
outfit of charms which I bought from his relatives after his
death; they were afraid to touch it, and for another Dayong to

use it is taboo of the worst kind. Such charms are usually buried with the practitioner, but this old fellow evidently did not have a very large practice, and, at his death, he was somewhat neglected. One of the charms is a stone in which an active imagination might trace a resemblance to the hand or foot of an animal; the sorrowing relatives told me, with awe and bated breath, that it was given to their uncle by a spirit on the top of a mountain, and that it was the foot of a dragon, one of the most powerful resources of the Dayong pharmacopœia.

Companions to the stories of visits to the regions below the earth are stories of visits to the world above the skies, to which adventurous heroes climb either by vines or ropes, which dangle suddenly in front of them, or by means of lofty trees. "Jack and the Bean Stalk" is a parallel story in our own folk-lore. Sir Spencer St. John* gives a Dayak account of the introduction of rice among the Orang Iban, as they call them-selves, which states that " when mankind had nothing to eat but fruit and a species of fungus which grows round the roots of trees, a party of Ibans, among whom was a man named *Si Jura* (whose descendants live to this day in the village of Simpok) went forth to sea. They sailed on for a long time until they came to a place where they heard the distant roar of a large whirlpool, and, to their amazement, saw before them a huge fruit tree rooted in the sky and thence hanging down, with its branches touching the waves. At the request of his companions, Si Jura climbed among its boughs to collect the fruit, which was in abundance; when he got among the boughs, he was tempted to ascend the trunk and find how the tree grew in that position. On looking down he saw his companions making off with the boat loaded

* " Forests of the Far East," vol. I, p. 213.

KAYAN WOMEN.

with fruit ; there was nothing for him to do but go on climbing.
At length he reached the roots of the tree and found himself in
the country of the Pleiades [which the Dayaks call 'the seven
chained-stars']; when he stood upon the ground he met a man-
like being, whose name was Si Kira, and he went with him to
his house. For food Si Kira offered to him a mess of soft white
grains, and told him to eat. 'What, eat those little maggots?'
said Si Jura. 'They are not maggots, that is boiled rice,'
replied Si Kira, and he forthwith instructed him in the art of
planting, weeding, reaping, husking, and boiling rice.

"While Si Kira's wife was out, getting some water, Si Jura
peeped into one of the tall jars that were standing near by, and
looking straight through the bottom of it, he could see his father's
house and all his brothers and sisters sitting around talking.  His
spirits were much depressed at the remembrance of the home that
perhaps he should never see again, and instead of eating he wept.
Si Kira at once saw what was the matter, and assured him that
he would arrange everything satisfactorily for him; then Si
Jura fell to and ate a hearty meal, and afterwards he was given
three kinds of rice, and Si Kira further instructed him how to
fell the jungle, burn it, then take the omens from the birds
before planting, and when he harvested to hold a feast.  By means
of a long rope Si Jura was lowered down to the earth again, close
to his father's house.  From his visit to the Pleiades the Dayaks
learned all that they know about farming, and, what is more, to
this day the Pleiades themselves tell them when to begin farming, for, according to their position in the sky in the morning
and evening, they cut down the jungle, burn, plant, and reap."

I think there can be no doubt that Si Kira bestowed a great
blessing on the Dayaks when he gave them rice ; but I am very

sure that he saddled them with a dire affliction when he introduced to them the omen-birds ; more procrastination, failure of expeditions, and exasperation of soul can be laid to the score of these birds than to anything else on earth. There is hardly an undertaking, however slight, that can be begun without first consulting these wretched birds. Yet it is hardly to be wondered at, that all tribes should hold the birds to be little prophets of the jungle, dashing across man's path, at critical moments, to bless or to ban. In the deep jungle, which at high noon is as silent as "sunless retreats of the ocean," gay-plumaged birds are not sitting on every bough singing plaintive, melodious notes; such lovely pictures exist solely in the mind of the poet or of him who has never visited the tropics. In the thick tangle of leaves and branches overhead, the larger birds are seen with difficulty, even after considerable practice, and the smaller birds appear as but a flash of light, as they dart through the interlacing palms and vines ; the apparition, with its sudden gleam and instant disappearance, starts the impulse to make a wish, as when we see a star shoot across the heavens. This same natural and almost irresistible impulse, which we have all experienced, I suggest as one of the explanations of the tendency of the Bornean mind to accept the birds as the intelligent forerunners of good or ill. These unsophisticated natives wander forth with some wish in their hearts, and should a bird of the right species (for not all birds are omen-birds) cross their path, the fulfilment of their wishes is established beyond a doubt by its mere appearance, and it is to be feared (for they are mortal) that if they do not want to see the bird—well, there are none so blind as those who won't see. When it comes to taking omens for such an important event as the planting of rice, or for going on the warpath, then the ceremony extends over ten days or two weeks, and the opinion of the small barking deer also must be consulted ; furthermore, the whole household is under the ban of a taboo, or *permantang*, as they call it, and the people must all stay indoors while the three men who are appointed as searchers are abroad on their omen-seeking errand. So firm is their trust in the wisdom of the birds that even if they have worked for months at a clearing they will abandon it and never plant it, if the omens at the time of sowing be unfavorable. Certain birds must be seen on the right hand to be favorable, while others are most propitious when they soar overhead, or give a shrill cry on the left ; on more than one occasion, when traveling in native canoes, a bird which ought to have appeared on the right has been seen on the left, and, to my utter bewilderment, without a word the boat has been swung round in the stream so as to bring to the right what was on the left, thus slyly fabricating a bad omen into a good one, and for some distance we have gone in the opposite direction, but now with highly favorable omens. When they conclude that the bird has forgotten his warning or lost sight of us, the boat has been again turned, fate has been deceived, and we journey on as before. Once our whole party of eight or ten boats had to pull up at the bank and walk through the jungle for a quarter of a mile or so to make a bothersome white-headed hawk think that he had mistaken the object of our expedition. When a favorable bird has been seen, a fire of chips is at once built on the bank of the river, thereby letting the bird know that his kind attention has been appreciated. Fire is always the go-between of man and the birds, or any of the spirits ; it forms an important part in the cere-monies of consecration and absolution, and by means of fire a man may break through a taboo, or *permantang*. Should a man have a fruit-tree, for instance, which he wishes to protect, he places about it several cleft sticks with stones thrust in the clefts, and the stones are told to guard the tree and afflict with dire diseases any pilferer of the fruit. Now, should a friend of the owner see this sign of *permantang* and yet wish some of the fruit, let him but build a fire and commission the fire to tell the stones that he is a friend of the owner, and that it is all right if he takes the fruit; then, when the fire is burnt out, the fruit may be taken with impunity. In the ceremony of naming a child, the sacrificial pig is touched with a fire brand before it is harangued by the Dayong, or medicine man; and to determine whether or not the chosen name be propitious, the strip of rattan which has been used on the fire-saw to obtain the sacred fire, is bent into a loop until its ends just meet; it is then set on fire in the middle and allowed to burn through. If the two pieces thus made are of uneven length the name is good; if they are both the same length another name must be selected. The ashes from this burning are made into a paste and smeared on the child's forehead just before it is deluged with a bowl of cold water, and the name is made public for the first time. It is strange what a similarity exists in different races relative to this ceremony of giving a name. Why water should be used to confirm the rite, they cannot themselves explain, except by saying that it is a custom handed down to them from their grandfathers and their great-great-grandfathers. It can hardly have suggested itself to the minds of the Borneans as an element of purification and cleansing; to their mind water does not possess these properties. Water is good to drink when you are thirsty, and refreshing to bathe in when you are

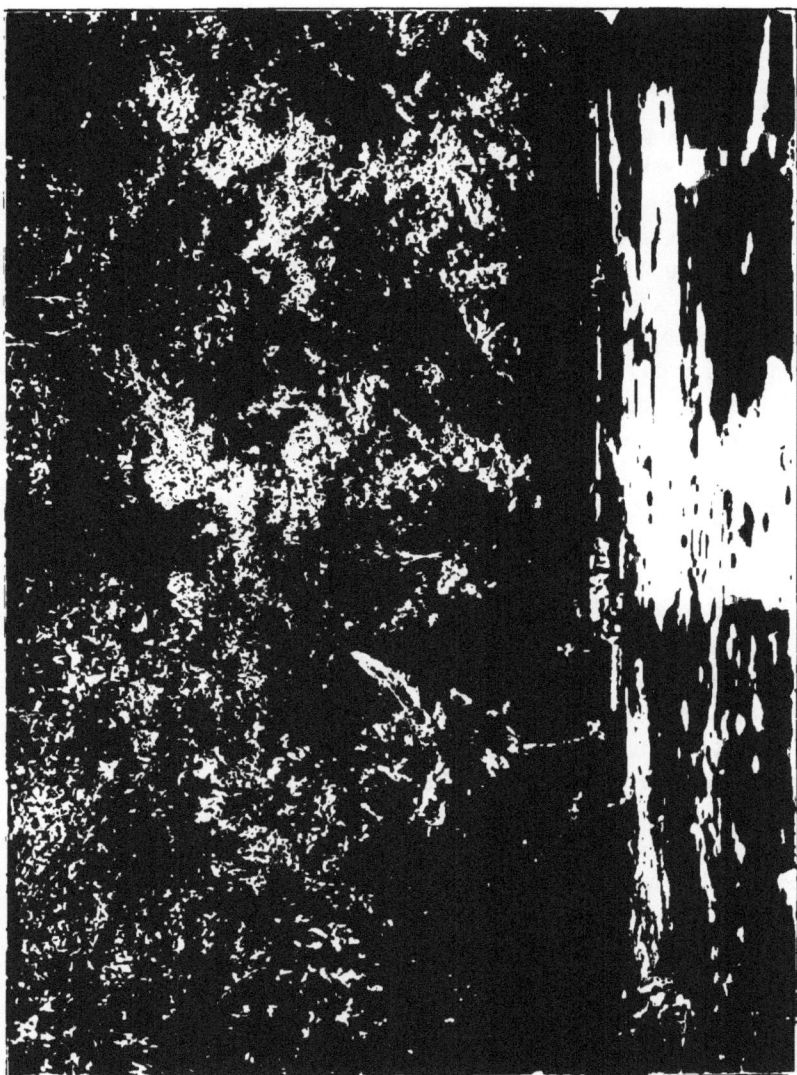

A Scene on the Dapoi River.

hot, that is all; dirt has no horrors to the Bornean mind, and after a plunge in the river has refreshed the body, the Kayan, Dayak, Kenyah, Sibop, or whatever the tribe, will put on the same dirty waist-cloth or cotton jacket that has never known soap, and has seldom if ever been nearer the water than when on the back of its owner. Perhaps it is that water is symbolic of life and motion; the river is always moving, it murmurs and talks to itself, a draft of its coolness and a plunge into its embrace adds new life to man; why should it not be the giver of life? In almost all the native languages of Borneo the word for water and river is the same; even when water is brought up into the house it is still the river, and when they drink, they drink the river; when they boil their rice they boil in the river, and when they name their children they pour the river over them. Many subtribes or households take their name from the river on which they live, as, for instance, the Long Patas who live, or used to live, at the mouth of the Pata river (Long meaning junction of one river with another), the Long Kiputs, the Long Lamas, and many others that might be named, including the whole tribe of the Kayans, who take their name from the great Kayan river which empties into the sea on the East coast. If a river that is new to them be visited, the spirits of that stream must be always propitiated lest they resent the intrusion and drown the visitor. It is the custom among the Bukits, one of the most primitive tribes, for the youths, when they reach the bank of a new river, to divest themselves of every article of clothing, save a chaplet of leaves, which they twist from the vines near at hand; then crouching at the edge of the water, they toss some personal ornament, such as a brass ear-ring or a bright bead, far out into mid-stream, and at the same instant scoop up a handful of the water; gazing earnestly into the few drops which they hold in their palm, they invoke the spirits of the river to protect them, and implore permission to enter the new territory. Not until this rite is completed would they dare to bathe in the stream.

To revert to the subject of names; from all that I have read, and from personal observation, it seems that all Borneans recognize the sanctity of names; of this we may find traces among all the primitive people of the earth. Before the formal ceremony of naming a child, for instance, has been performed, the child has no recognized place in the community, and a mother in enumerating her children would never think of mentioning one that had died before it was named, even though it had lived a year. Before the ceremony, the intended name is known to no one except the parents, and, for them to mention it, is strictly *permantang* until the river water has been poured on the child's head. A Kayan will never tell you his name, but when asked he invariably turns to some one sitting near him and asks him to pronounce the name which to the owner is ineffable. For a man to mention the name of his dead father or mother is a reckless flying in the face of providence. After a serious illness the name should be changed and never uttered again, lest the evil spirits revisit their victim; under a new name they will be likely to pass him by. On one occasion, recognizing a man that I had seen on a former visit, but, at the moment forgetting his name, I enquired what it was; the name, however, struck me as entirely unfamiliar. He afterward acknowledged that he had been very sick since I last saw him and now bore a new name; only the assurance that the spirits could not harm him through a white man induced him at last to whisper to me his former name. This change of name to deceive the fates extends even to inanimate objects, and to animals which are to be caught or trapped. When hunting for camphor, the name of the object of their search must be never mentioned; it is always spoken of as "the thing that smells." Even all the instruments, which they use in collecting the valuable drug, have fanciful names, while the searchers talk in a language invented solely for those who collect camphor. Unless they conform to all these requirements, the camphor crystals, which in this particular variety are found only in the crevices of the wood, will elude them and their search be fruitless. When the people go *Tuba-fishing*, which consists of poisoning the stream with the juice of the Tuba root, and thus stupefying the fish and making them rise to the surface, where they can be easily caught in nets or speared, they never say that they are going after fish, but after the leaves which float down stream.

These and many other customs relative to the naming of things are all founded on the same idea of the potency and mysticism inherent in a name, which may be found in the legends of the old Egyptians, wherein the power of the great king and god *Ra* depended on the fact that no one knew his real name, until Isis by stratagem got it from him; and forthwith his power left him. It was this same idea that prevented the Hebrew from ever speaking the name of the Most High; it is probably the same thought which prompts the Japanese to change a person's name after death lest by mentioning the one known during life the spirit of the dead should be recalled from the other world.

The downfall of the god *Ra* brings to mind another superstition of which I have noticed a remnant among the Borneans also, the power of working charms with the saliva. When the great god Ra became so old that he no longer had control of his lower jaw, Isis collected some of his saliva which dropped upon the ground below his throne, and mixing it with clay, made a snake of it. (I quote from the "Turin Papyrus," of which Mr. EDWARD CLODD gives a translation in his recent and valuable little book called "Tom Tit Tot.") This snake Isis left in Ra's path ; as he passed by, it bit him, and to relieve him of his agony Isis persuaded him that the only thing to be done was to tell her his true name that she might drive out the pain from his bones. This he finally did, and with disastrous results. I instance this to show the antiquity of the superstition that the saliva is potent as an ingredient of charms ; the Kayans illustrate this, in the manner whereby they elude an evil spirit which may have been following them on a journey on the river. They build a small archway of boughs on the bank just before they arrive at their destination. Underneath this arch, they build a fire and, in single file, all pass under, stepping over the fire and spitting into it as they pass ; by this act they thoroughly exorcise the evil spirits and emerge on the other side free from all baleful influence. Another instance, is where they are throwing aside the signs of mourning for the dead ; during the period of mourning they may not cut their hair nor shave their temples, but as soon as the mourning is ended by the ceremony of bringing home a newly-taken head, the barber's knife is kept busy enough. As every man leaves the barber's hands, he gathers up the hair, and, spitting on it, murmurs a prayer to the evil spirits not to harm him. He then blows the hair out of the verandah of the house.

All these parallelisms, in the modes of thinking, among men

in far removed quarters of the earth, do not, I think, necessarily imply that there has been a transmission of thought from one race to the other, but that there is a certain round of thought through which the brain leads us, and in development we must all have followed along the same path. Some races have made more rapid strides than others, possibly owing to natural surroundings, and in their strides have left the others centuries behind. Almost within the memory of our grandfathers, in this country, witches were burned, and from this there is only a step back to the Dayong of Borneo. Indeed, whosoever sees these people and lives with them their everyday life, must regard them, after a not very long time, merely as backward pupils in the school of life. Let me say in conclusion, that he would have an unresponsive heart that could not feel linked in a bond of fellowship with these people, and that God has made of only one blood all nations of the earth, when he hears a Bornean mother crooning her child to sleep with words identical in sentiment with " Rock-a-bye Baby,"—what though the mother's earlobes are elongated many an inch by heavy copper rings, her arms tattooed to the elbow, and her blackened teeth filed to points. Once upon a time I heard a Kayan mother soothing her little baby to sleep, and the words of the lullaby which I learned are as follows :—

From the River's mouth the birds are straying,
And the Baiyo's topmost leaves are swaying ;
    The little chicks cheep,
    Now my little one sleep,
For the black house-lizard, with glittering eye,
And the gray-haired Laki Laieng are nigh !
    Sleep, dear little one, sleep !

For those philologically inclined I append the original :—

Lung koh madang Manoh
Migieong ujong Baiyo
Mensip anak Yap
Lamate Telyap, Telyap abing,
Lamate Laki Laieng oban!
                    Ara we we ara!

www.ingramcontent.com/pod-product-compliance
Lightning Source LLC
Chambersburg PA
CBHW032137080426
42733CB00008B/1112